BATTLE DRESS

ALSO BY KAREN SKOLFIELD

Frost in the Low Areas

BATTLE DRESS

poems

KAREN SKOLFIELD

W. W. Norton & Company

Independent Publishers Since 1923

New York | London

For information about permission to reproduce selections from this book,
write to Permissions, W. W. Norton & Company, Inc.,
500 Fifth Avenue, New York, NY 10110

For information about special discounts for bulk purchases, please contact
W. W. Norton Special Sales at specialsales@wwnorton.com or 800-233-4830.

Manufacturing by Sheridan
Book design by JAM Design
Production manager: Lauren Abbate

Library of Congress Cataloging-in-Publication Data

Names: Skolfield, Karen, author
Title: Battle Dress : poems/Karen Skolfield
Description: First edition. | New York : W. W. Norton & Company, [2019]
Identifiers : LCCN 2019006960 | ISBN 9781324003014 (paperback)
Classification: LCC PS3619.K64 A6 2019 | DDC 811/.6—dc23
LC record available at https://lccn.loc.gov/2019006960

W. W. Norton & Company, Inc., 500 Fifth Avenue, New York, N.Y. 10110
www.wwnorton.com

W. W. Norton & Company Ltd., 15 Carlisle Street, London W1D 3BS

1 2 3 4 5 6 7 8 9 0

FOR FELIX, DENNIS, WALKER

CONTENTS

BATTLE DRESS

Enlist: *Origin < German*, to court, to woo

Perhaps with a desk between,
some chaste space, the recruiter leaning
forward, warm bodies on the other side.

Of the teenagers present
one will lie about her age,
one will eat bananas to make weight,

one pull herself from small-town quicksand.
Lace the hands behind the head,
look good in a uniform, look nonchalant.

Army doesn't take everyone,
maybe you, maybe not; lose 10 pounds,
no back talk, straight-spined, clear-eyed,

more than anything in your sad life
this matters; memorize the ranks,
don't act smart, go on long runs,

carry a pack, push-ups wouldn't hurt,
don't get pregnant, don't wet the bed,
first things they check.

Don't lie, but mark "no"
as much as you can, maybe a little more.
To be added to a list or catalog,

to see one's name nestled
among other names, included,
individual but part of, how an engine

. . .

won't run with a part misplaced,
how the lug nut informs the wheel.
Takes all kinds, some love KP,

some the motor pool, surveillance,
fire support, supply specialist,
infantry from the Latin for *children*.

You'll learn to work together, that's how
the Army is, someone's got to be
the firing pin, someone else the trigger.

On Veterans Day, My Daughter Wishes Me Happy Veterinarians Day

The sound of explosives disrupts
the species memory of migration.
Young ducks huddle at the burning ponds.
They'd fly, but where? Magnetic north
a confusion in the air, tracers falling to the ground.
The horses, even the battle trained,
wheel in confusion. The simple whites of their eyes.
My sergeant called what I did with a handgun
the needless slaughter of worms. He said
Skolfield, you're a crime against fishing.
Early in the morning,
my daughter's hair an irregular nest.
The peeping of fledglings.
In my hands a bowl, the silverware serrated.
What springs from those hands is a bludgeon of doves.

Double Arm Transplant

Even grafted limbs sigh
when the rains come.
The hands, those twin divining rods,
may tremble in the presence
of an old love. Now they're the arms
of a veteran. The hair that grows
from the arms a different shade.
Since the transplant he writes left-handed.
He waits for the hands to reveal
their previous life as farmer or electrician.
By a piano he pauses to see
if the wrists rise to the music.
If the knuckles love the baseball.
If the fist curls in anger. Before:
did he drum his fingers on the desk?
Was the salute quite so crisp?
On its own, the pinky angles to the teacup.
It's the giver of these arms speaking
whenever he debones a fish or juggles.
Every time a tennis ball comes down
it sits in the palm for a moment,
then rises again.

Grenade: *Origin* < *OFr.* pomme-grenate

Weight in the hand, inert as a seed
waiting to unlatch, encasement
before the cleaving, from asleep
to awake, from attached to singular
how a seed case splits and reveals
such tenderness but also its power,
roots cracking rock, stem shaking
the earth. A seed makes itself known,
prepares the earth for its own good work,
changes the landscape. Glossy,
harboring within, the rounded shape
sarcotesta as of the testicle which in itself
means *witness*, embryo like no other,
willing to feed upon itself, of varying size,
astringency over sweetness.
Without tending reverts to its wild form.
In mythology, every seed a month
of hell for the mother, the daughter,
her daughter's daughters
along the generations. In every war,
the same recognizable hunger.
Fruit of the dead, from living to not living,
also fruit of fertility, from one to many,
the names of the dead ripening.
How the arm extends, the palm opens,
the red pulp within, the perfect arc.
What is sown cannot be called back.
We say *bearing fruit* and it is borne.

The Throwing Gap

Because so many recruits threw like girls
we had to be tested before moving on
to live grenades, helmets chalked
with "P" or "F," or was it "Y" or "N,"
was it "XX" which meant bad,
"XY" which meant good, with a helmet
who could tell what was being written,
chalk in the hand of a man. We willed
our arms to be boys, our shoulders
brutal and male, we thought of torsos
and hands that had beaten or punched
or strangled or slapped or headlocked
women that were us or looked
like us and we wanted that strength.
We did not want the tenderness
we saw in certain men. We did not want
their baby soothing, pot stirring,
back rubbing, dishwashing gestures.
If they owned ride-on lawnmowers
we did not want that, nor book readers,
nor lovers of cats and wine and appetizers;
if they had hobbies let it be catcalling,
the gutting and skinning of mammals,
the flaying of fish. Let dominion be shown
by the men we wanted to be,
let pianos be lifted, bench-press two bills,
let it be football even if the QB
was so often the slightest of them,
let any dress shoes languish in the closet
until Sundays and funerals. Make us male

for this moment, the thickened thorax,
the height; make it come with a temper,
make us want to destroy whatever displeased,
have us piss on lawns as demarcation.
Whatever someone else has built,
make us want to knock over.
Let us say pussy, pussy, pussy
and hate ourselves, let us see those
who lack strength and crush them,
let us beer can to the forehead,
let us drink and punch our own selves
and then the mirrors and the windows
and whatever may reflect like a stranger's
or spouse's or child's pinpricked eyes
which are our own eyes let it be failure
that drives us or the fear of it or someone
who said pussy pussy pussy while lighting
our boy hair on fire or unbuckling the buckle
let us not ever show compassion for that boy
let us take a grenade and say *hell yes*
and play with the pin and cannot wait
to violence and let us love vengeance
let it be the one thing we truly love.
Let us throw these grenades so far
that the drill sergeant says
God, seeing hand grenades thrown
like that gives me a hard-on
and we who are now male will laugh
at the rightness of it and we will say *Me too*.

Private, PV2, Private First Class

From the Latin *privare*: to deprive,
fullsleep and showers, homethoughts,
othergender except that one dance
stomping in bivvies and combat boots,
most of us decked in Birth Control Glasses
woooo those things worked.

Also *privus*: individual,
from *pro*: in front of, night guard,
front line, outside the wire, patrol,
protect, privilege, *privet*—but how
did the word go from trimmed hedges
to us when we were so rootless.

Camo paint gumming up our pores,
jungle palette: vineknot, humus, treetangle.
Pvt. Morales painting cheekbones
like Escher drawings.
If viewed one way we were women;
if another darkbirds winging into light.

This was two years before
we knew what was blowing our way.
Promotion to specialist. Base change.
The shift of Desert Storm:
camo to clay, stone, shadow, sand.

Soldier Rendered as All Five Types of Sand Dunes

Crescentic

Most common and thus easiest
to hide among, gravel swept,
grassthin, low crawl, creepalong,
identical sway and leaf, palmate,
camouflage, among many
one soldier one civilian
shopping in a market

Linear

Sinuous, bidirectional
as in a man looking both ways
sensing another
behind him, intent drawn,
the senses become sharpened
in times of war, most often isolated,
strung thin, and if two converge
one swallows whole the other

Star

Slipfaced, radiant, heart refusing
to detach, O brothers upward
leaping, eyes all around
battle buddy, latrine even,
meaning more when dusk
growing upward, tallest thing on earth

Dome

Circular the reasoning of war,
no fools, they've seen
political cartoons, had the joke
enacted on their bodies. The soldier
forwards a .gif of M16 casings
turning gold, cast into pockets
of the whiterich, set on repeat,
mouthgrit they learn to laugh through,
on patrol stands at the
upwind margin of sandsea,
horizon scans the nothing, which means
not yet

Parabolic

Blowout, hairpin, crested,
elongate arms for pushaway,
stormsifted, ragecrossed,
horn of the bull, held back
in part and fixed in place,
the rest in migration
impossible to sitstill
with the windburn, even just
the sound of it, remember?

Open your empty, blameless hands,
your mouth where the knives hide,
the folds where the bullets might live.
Prove you're mammalian by twisting
your neck a mere 160 degrees,
180 if you're under thirty. It's the seven
vertebrae that give you away.
Even giraffes have that number.
Even the smallest of the squirrels.
Your hands passed down to you by seals.
Bones from the bat's impossible wings.
Touching the forehead signals humility
and servitude. It signals that in a flash,
you'd bend to shine his shoes,
marry his ridiculous son.
Chain of command the old
trickle-down economics,
with you standing on the bottom step,
waiting for pennies to rain.
On his collar a bird of prey
with its whopping 14 vertebrae
and 270 degrees of freedom to the neck.
Don't you wish your camouflage
let you blend into the barracks?
Don't you wish his eyes
would go somewhere else?
When saluting, the arm should make
an audible snap, as if the bones were giving.

While your hand's up there,
scratch your eyebrow.
It's itchy, and bothers you more
and more these days.

Combined Plow and Gun Patent, 1862

After that misbirthed blast I redesigned
with muzzle tip away, though the Lord
was watching: the grapeshot raged past
one ear and scared the crows off the corn.
Now the muzzle points downfield,
always at the ready. You can hook up
the oxen pair, sure, but I'd advise against it.
Abby says this goes contrary to the Bible
with its cheek-turning, but these are difficult times.
If God had wanted to change the pillar of salt
back into Lot's wife, He could have done.
The plagues of Egypt croaked through
and then were gone. If the Nile River's
still blood, no one mentions it.
The idea came in church: God wants me
to stitch farming and warring back together
for this small time. It's the firstborn males
dying in such numbers. Even in the Bible,
the wending of wartime and peace. The plow
not meant always to be cleaved from the sword.
That blood of begetting. The earth wiped clean.
In the postdiluvian world, Noah understood
how the drownings were counterpoint
to his salvation. Make no mistake:
first God made the dove, then He sent the rains.

"The Great Sacrifice of the Romans on Undertaking a War"

after the engraving in The Faiths of the World, *1857*

Not to be dismissive, but the Romans
aren't sacrificing much:
a pig, a ram, some flasks of wine,
one guy's holding what might be a pie
but it's token more than tribute.
The scene: festive and homoerotic
with bare-chested men twirling axes,
so butch they count double. Ankle bracelets,
strappy sandals, well-muscled legs.
Of course this is before the war,
bench-pressing babes contemplating a win.
Even the giving feels good, the extra ox
feeding luscious men like themselves.
Someone's pulled out a curvy instrument
and is blowing that thing. Two others
raise the long horns to their lips.
The music so upbeat a conga line
of animals is posing hooves and shanks
and the men dig it, banners in the distance,
a little antebellum bump and grind.
No women, no surprise: no *joie de la guerre*
from the ladies, and besides their sons,
what would the women have to give?
In poems I count the years until my son
registers for the draft. I know him:
He'll boogie to the post office, sign his card.
He's down to six years, a number which,
in Roman numerals, looks like one
not-quite man beside the V for victory.

Anticipate Gunshots in the Second Half of the Play

Real gunshots? my son asks.
I say, just the sound.
Well that will be pretty loud, he says.
When's the last time you heard gunshots? I ask.
This morning, he says.
Suddenly I remember the little pop pop
during his soccer game.
From the rifle range, I say.
I almost couldn't play, he says, it was so loud.
Although in truth
it had sounded like snapping twigs,
an odd atmospheric moment
funneled our way. Still air
and our boys in gray jostling
for the ball against Granby's boys in blue.
The blue and gray part was not
a thing I'd think of until the play,
and those gunshots, in the distance.
Will the sound bother you? I ask.
Mom, it's *Les Mis*, he says,
but it will be loud, believe me.
You know I was in the military, I say.
The lights have dimmed and if his eyes
are rolling I can't see them.
He leans over, wants to tell me
something but the curtains
have parted to the cruelty
of guards, the singing of men
in chains.

Rifle: *verb, noun*

Carry away the spiral grooves,
steal the bore. The fourteenth century
armed to ransack, of Germanic origin.

Shoulder the intent. Let the French
middle their way in, ask them
what they saw. What weapon

scratched, we're up to 1770,
the origin defined and other.
Artillery akin to steal. Carry away

what's explosive, the plunder term.
The soldier bored and away carry
the first known use.

Oh 1937, what propelled you, what
weaponed term and transitive.
Automatic the shoulder and arms,

the plural of soldier automatic,
sawing its bored way in.
Steal, that's the term, the spiral back,

the define of force, hunting.
Propel, call it hunting.
Call it automatic, as in used and spiraling.

Call it a piece. The soldier obsolete
and used, perhaps. Hunting,
how term your automatic bore,

. . .

the barrel cut and bored and you,
as a ball, made plural, spiraling,
propelled with great force or speed.

Army SMART Book: "Small-arms fire may sound like mosquitoes"

Then those are the scariest fucking mosquitoes
ever. Mosquitoes. Who told you that?
Some writer? Mosquitoes big enough
to carry off your soul. Mosquitoes the size
of a dinner plate, size of an exit wound.
People who say mosquitoes
are back troops hearing it in the distance.
It's the patrols outside the wire
that worry about your "mosquitoes."
I'd call it more hornet, or jacket zipper.
Crack, hiss. Someone pissing in his pants.
A man snapping his fingers
as if he wanted you to look at him.

Saltpeter

It's what's for dinner. The Army
sprinkles it on everything,
well, when the males go through the line.
It's in a big jar with holes in the lid,
right next to where they dish out
the main course. Females don't need it.
Females don't get hard-ons
when the wind blows
or stops or starts again. Females—
they probably care about sex,
yeah, but not the same way,
and saltpeter doesn't make a difference.
In the old days it was raping and pillaging.
Now we get saltpeter.
You can taste it, especially on the eggs.
Not salty, like you'd think.
More savory, like some herb.
Helps the males on watch
stay focused instead of thinking
about getting laid. I'm telling you,
the whole platoon has talked about this.
We take showers together and all,
so it's probably good. We've done gym,
sports, whatever, but first thing in the morning
would be a lot of wood. I've heard
once you go off the stuff, a guy's body
has to make up for all those missed erections.
I'm taking a week off just in case.
Kanakia said he'd need a month.
Nester said he'd need a year.
God, like it's some fucking competition.

Soldiers' 'Fun' Photo with Flag-Draped Coffin Sparks Outrage

Anyone who spends the day lifting bodies
in the air needs an outlet, they said
in their defense. Of course they know
they'll have their turn, some future war,
the bullet before the bullet's sound.
Shrapnel against bone's imperfect shield.
The Honor Guard was privilege.
But weren't they human? Don't others
get to smile at their work? In the office,
boxes of new flags folded into triangles.
A warehouse of body bags in case.
They did their jobs. Don't say they didn't.
In the photo, men embrace
and look surprised to see another man
in their arms. One looks on approvingly.
One crosses her eyes. A tongue stuck out,
some rabbit ears, one soldier sleeps
against the coffin's edge,
one lies down in front as if they'd rolled
the coffin to the beach. It's where we work,
they said. Where else to take a picture
of our group? We meant no disrespect.
The body in the coffin long past caring.
The family would be thanking us now
instead of all this bad press,
if giggling woke the dead.

Classic Green Army Figures Give Up Guns for Yoga

for Dan Abramson, creator of "Yoga Joes"

At the apex of the pose
those little green arms
feel the pop of little green tendons.
Satisfaction of the stretch.
Whoever said lay down
your weapons has never
laid down weapons in quite this way,
plasticine, the arms forming a letter,
V for victory, L for lion hearted,
Y for the question Why this war.
The forever warrior pose.
Soldiers, be small and green
in your work, pliant everlasting,
road of the rising sun;
form the body into another animal,
the crane and hare in salutation,
cobra at the bend, be the hunter
or the hunted, glide of limbs
into the posture of the half-hero.
When the yoga soldiers
breathe out, the fresh tang
of the newly minted upon them.
In basic training, how we stretched
on our racks and slept
symmetrically, savasana,
the held corpse stance
of our night's sleeping.
Bound angle, Bikram triangle,

the swing of legs over
the bunk's edge. On waking,
the stretch of limbs, that extra minute
climbing back into our bodies.

The Sentry Responds

cricketsong
       brown as
soldiers' shirts
       we sound
dusky
       roughskinned
nomoon
       canvas smell
boots on
       exhausted
they sleep
       as they fall
begrimed
       sunsalted
let me tell you
       firstwatch
how notcity
       dark on dark
not frightened
       not exactly
but wary
       how patrol
unseeing
       the quickened ears
comfort
       of rifle
from the brush
       a voice *You ladies*
can really snore
       drill sergeant

whispers as if
      equals
and I
      not even an I
ordered silent
      ordered *lookaway*
which I do
      as if the trees
held secrets
      the grisaille
of darkness
      he panthers
into tents
      feels for
rifles unsecured
      me their sentry
but fighting sleep
      they knew
how a man
      might prowl
how a woman
      failing
that I was no
      protection at all

Army SMART Book: Identification Tags, with Silencers

The Army—look how it loves,
writing your name over
and over.

Obsessed, maybe.
Worn like shame like
the Army's your man

but he's hit you.
Hidden like a rib
cracked beneath the shirt.

Army tee itself the color
of an old bruise
fading.

One tag toe-looped,
the other to wedge between
the teeth.

How it would sound, little
pop of glory, the dog tag
clicking into place.

Just another soldier
kicking your name
back into your mouth.

CNN Report: Rise in Sexual Assaults, Reprisals in the Military (2016)

It's not just the stars
these last mornings
I failed to see.
No light pollution.
My flashlight
the walk's metronome.
Consider how no one takes
the stories of stars seriously
these days. The journalist
asked me what I thought
of my time in the military.
It's the motion of a deer
that catches my eye,
makes me look back and see
a sunrise I almost missed.
Blazing and violent,
and once it's gone,
no evidence it ever existed.

Why I Never Wrote About the Army

Four hours a night
and we slept with our rifles,
strap twined around skinny forearms,
brass and ammo locked away
and catch on safety.
Drill Sergeant Robinson warned
that if he snuck
into our shelter halves
and nabbed a rifle,
why, we'd be pushing
Fort Dix off the map.
We laughed, our voices too high,
our camouflage paint cracking
into frightened, toothy grins.
He held a rifle over his head:
"For the next eight weeks,
this is your boyfriend!"
I thought, "girlfriend."

No one in my platoon
breathed a word the nights
Alexis crept into my bunk.
After full-pack road marches I'd wake
screaming from a charley horse,
animal sounds ragged
and out of touch with the night.
They were glad I had someone
to smooth my cramped muscles
and shut me up. And everyone
was so far from home.

Latest rumor was that
a girl in the next platoon
was getting discharged
for being queer
and I asked my ranger buddy
to point her out
but she couldn't, and me dying
to know what one looked like.

Due to Historical Accuracy, Hazards Are Present

—U.S. Army Heritage Trail, Carlisle, PA

Take another loop if you want
to jump wars, IEDs daisy-chained
in some cornfield's center.

Thick middle of the M18 tank destroyer
guarding the only weeds
landscapers can't reach.

That we won the Revolution:
a marvel, footprints bloodier
over every mile marched.

In the WWII barracks a moving body
triggers a voice that's eager to tell
the favorite C-rations of soldiers.

Have I been separated from my unit?
In the parachute jump simulator,
I miss the drop zone twice.

My family's in Massachusetts.
Dog walkers skirt the soccer fields
and a Huey's blades bound by wire.

Within the WWI Trench exhibit,
a visitor tries out the Aid Station,
surgical table the length of a child.

. . .

Those dangling legs.
He's so good at being perfectly still.
Those who feel lucky

may guess their way to safety.
Barbed wire in a ring,
a mortar crater softened by erosion.

Two Pennsylvania children
zigzag the mock minefield,
triggering all the bells.

Metal crooning of World War I
now prefabricated and accordioned.
What wind does when
it touches wire, unspooled
demarcation, the no-man's whistle.
In other times how they might
sing while working, *sotto voce*,
the diminutive breath.
Ring upon ring of barbery
pinging into blackness
where in the distance
there once were cattle.
What a civilian might see
as the posturing of shame:
soldiers begloved, working
in darkness, their very
faces turned away.

We Invaded Two Weeks Later

It's so humid in Panama
that the mosquitoes drowse midday,
their appetite for blood quiet
until the earth tips a notch.
Women wear *mola* art
over their breasts, strips of fabric
layered with careful stitches
blending into bright cloth.
The women sew family stories,
a white branch for marriage,
a bird for happiness and wealth,
a snake anchored to their nipples
to prevent miscarriage.

When the soldiers come to shop
at the women's stands, the senoritas
use their English—*pretty, pretty.*
They touch my hair
and pull gently at my one earring.
Leche, they say, my drinkable skin.

One shy girl shares
her smile with me.
Her eyes blue
among dark-eyed people,
signaling she
is a soldier's daughter.
Each day I buy something
from her, a *mola* stitched
by her small hands,

rings of fresh pineapple,
a coin purse decorated
with green feathers.
Each day I give her Panamanian
balboas minted in Denver.
When the planes fly by
she laughs and waits for my laughter.
I empty my pockets of bright balboas.

The one comfort: before,
war had no name,
the rocks unburdened
by history and maybe the sticks
not so pointed. No one drilled,
no one steadied himself against a tree.
The powder existed only for fireworks,
the arrow for the hare. Trenches
known only for drainage. The fields
unsown with salt, the wells sweet,
the barn unburned, the untroubled
daughter. If there were hen's eggs
the shells were whole; anger lived
as a tiny thing, size of a moth,
capable only of short distances.
In gatherings of men out came the flute,
a drum eager for callused hands.
The fist opened up for the plow,
the long rows of cabbages.
Akin to the Old English *wiersa,*
meaning it can always get worse.
The first battle tactic: surround
a village, have the horns of soldiers
wake the slumbering who,
for one glad moment,
can't place the sound.

Poem with the Moment the Infantry Unit Is Given Clearance to Shoot Children

As in, of course you may use the bathroom; why are you asking?
As in, here's the worst thing I'm ever going to whisper in your ear.
A breath of almonds and talc, not decay, as one might expect.
"Is Given": Passive voice, the arms turned to noodles, the body
drooped against the couch. Finger languid to the trigger. Soldiers
report sudden cases of synesthesia: for every round of gunfire, the
bloom of purple. *Not red?* asks the therapist. *Not black?* When the
therapist asks, the soldier sees green. As in, authorization, which
means to place a burning key in the palm of another. The radio
playing anything but love songs. The surprise of any desert is how
many colors exist if the eye can rest long enough, if the cones can
adjust. Imprimatur: let it be printed on the bookspine of soldier.
In peacetime, a man will give his life to push a child from the
path of a speeding bus. The tiniest skitter of movement, a door-
way brought to its knees. Permission from above: *Create within, a
driver with his eyes fixed to the horizon. Be the bus.*

Chevron: *Origin* < rafter, *also* goat

Just after the slick sleeve
of no insignia comes the rafter,
the rocker. In house parlance
the sistering of beams,
two women joined together.
In heraldry the chevronel,
first of the mountains,
a family crafted from hardship,
breath lost after the climb,
handscrabble, one soldier
reaching back to help the other
or letting boot after boot
use her cupped hands as the step.
Hard stripes: earned in the field.
Soft stripes: college courses,
some bubbles filled in,
good at essays but not much else.
A battle buddy has the six o'clock
and gives the snap-to
for sergeant stripes approaching.
Skew at the collar a cause for push-ups.
Don't let those things weigh you down,
Drill Sergeant said.
Blackened wingtips from Latin's *caper*,
the V-shape of a goat's horns.
Collective noun: a tribe of goats,
the trip, the drove, if there were safety
in numbers we'd be drowning in goats,
cloven hooves, sign of the unclean.
Oh *Capricorn*, most stubborn

of the Zodiac if left to roam
unherded, but in the goat's heart
the desire of domestication,
and with a pinky's-width rope
so willingly led.

Manassas

Even in sunlight the darkness mixed in—
the dark of pupils, black vacuum of our mouths,
open because we've forgotten to close them,
because it's no longer important. Because we're left
at the creek with our tongues circling a slip of water.
Because our bodies are dumb animals
that bleat like sheep, that die like sheep
with one thin, final scream that barely stirs the grass.
Because our bodies move on without us.

Listen. The ringing from the hills. A man stands
like a stone wall, crushes the red clover and brome
that bayonets the air. The eight-inch cannons,
plugged shut, carry an old heat within. A plastic
lens cap is lost on the field, and in the foreground,
tourists blink in and out of the wall of fog.

"You cannot be disciplined in great things and undisciplined in small things. There is only one sort of discipline—perfect discipline."

—GENERAL GEORGE S. PATTON JR.

"I hate having female recruits,"
Drill Sergeant Robinson told us.
"The males, I can break.
I break them down, build them
back up, then they do anything
for me. Females don't break."
The sadness in his voice
made us sad, too. We wanted
to break. Maybe we could fake
being good soldiers.
What would breaking look like,
for the females? Tears
we already knew how to do.

Army SMART Book: Inspirational Quotes (II)

"When your shot is exhausted, knock down the enemy with the stock of your rifle. If the rifle stock be broken, bite with your teeth."

—RUSSIAN MILITARY READER

Two stoppered rifles.
You hadn't guessed

she'd look like you.
Even the enjambment in

her eyes. Tiny breasts.
Jawcurve, waistsmall.

Fists that once were hands.
Perfect, exceptional teeth.

Bayonet: *Origin* < *from* Bayonne, France

Good river, or hill by the river,
the waters known especially
for their sweetness, gentle reeds,
rocky beds that do not need dredging.
In its most ancient spelling, *Baiona*,
the feminine, as of women bending
toward the water, raising it up.
Even the work by the river
felt light, skew of shore, children
playing on the rocks.
All light was good light by the river.
Those who know rivers know
how hard it is to be angry
in their presence. If the powder
and projectiles were low, what of it.
Of course there were knives
for the usual things. The butchering
went on, but nearer the town's center.
Scythes for the wheat.
What came of it was bread
thick-crusted and difficult,
the middle warm and yielding.

Third Platoon Learns Cover & Concealment

Our hair smelled of canvas and green.
Alexis sat cross-legged and touched
my cheekbone with one finger.

She paused as she scanned my face:
"light in the valleys, dark on the hills.
I swear, you look good in green."

I wove leaves into her helmet, tried
to stay still and shivered as she softened
the lines from brown to green.

We learned to move like shadows.
Muzzles pointed into the brush,
our small blackened hands flashed signals—

enemy ahead, take cover. Alexis
appeared beside me, whispered
"we're setting up an ambush."

Three women melted into the brush
on my right and panted slowly,
half drowsing in the June heat,

their eyes blinking beneath the leaves.
I wanted to tell her green could be painful,
how the ripeness of forests could crumble to earth.

Her hand rested inches from mine. Around us,
the smell of leaf mold curtained the forest,
and we waited for rain, or the footsteps of women.

Ode to Meals, Ready to Eat

Of dubious origin and uncertain
culinary background, of finely chopped
and extruded into pouch, of gelatinous
eminence, Chicken à la King.
The one meal never traded.
You get what you get and you don't
get upset, except dehydrated pork patty.
Bunkmate gets pork patty
and you get Chicken à la King,
she'll throw the big compliment:
That shit looks almost edible.
You offer her fruitcake.
She says, I'm thinking royalty.
She says, that King looks like he might
want to visit a few more of his subjects.
She says, God, I haven't gotten a letter in weeks.
She says, You did all right in the locker inspection
after I fixed your sock drawer, right?
The King's primacy of noodles,
blocky and proud, pinkish.
The divine right of salt.
Faint reminder of Sunday casseroles
made with canned soup.
You'd help your mom: shredding chicken,
adding frozen vegetables, working
the can opener and the soup, condensed,
which everyone knows
only a fool waters down.

Army SMART Book: M18A1 Claymore Mine

*The number of ways in which the claymore mine may be employed
is limited only by the imagination of the user.*

The perfect doorstop: heavy, unobtrusive.
Can be used to conk intruders on the head.
It won't go off accidentally, no worries,
it's not that kind of mine. While waiting
for the next war, it's a handy paperweight.
Sunk in the fish tank, over time it grows
a patina of algae and the gouramis give it kisses.
Look at the catfish whiskering the detonator well!
What they don't know won't hurt them.
Claymore mines are excellent for propping
the wobbly table, bookending, pounding nails.
Okay, pounding nails might be pushing it,
but it really is okay to scrape the windshield's ice.
Toddler can't reach the table? Planting roses?
Yes and yes. Your five-year-old can practice
sounding out the words "Front Toward Enemy."
Your teenager, forever noodling with things,
can admire the priming adapter, the simple
bowed front, the interior full of iron fragments,
as innocuous as a toolbox. In fact, a toolbox
is a nice place to store claymores. Or perhaps
the living room. This is a weapon that fits
into daily life. With the metal legs unfolded,
it looks like some old TV with rabbit ears.
There you sit, staring at the thing, wishing
someone else would change the channel.

The cows push through the gate while I'm trying to write about the military. Look at them! A whole herd, and none of them cares about the military. They're making a mess of the place: churning up snow, eating the rosebushes, trampling everything. They shouldn't be here while I'm trying to write about the military. These cows don't have a thought in their heads except following nose to tail, aiming for the bare grass beneath the trees. Because there's so many, it's impossible to tell who is leader. They're on their second circuit of my studio where I'm writing about the military, or trying to, except for the cows. Prey animals, their eyes to the sides of their heads, but you can tell they've gone complacent and don't know a thing about the military. The sounds out of their mouths might be complaints or praise, but it's certainly not about the military. Think for yourselves! I call to them. Their heads tip up and down in exactly the same way. To say they look alike would be an understatement.

Nurse Voted Best in SAC

Terrible headline, get it?
Strategic Air Command.

Get it? The instructor's voice
a nimble unrolling
of stockings,

a white cap starched.

Uh-huh, got it.
An exaggerated tug
to our camouflage collars,
the obedient laughter
of privates.

Oh, lord. The mistakes
a journalism student
could make.

And what if
I went in for the exam,
that nurse telling me
to disrobe?

I'd tremble. I'd do as I was told.

Most Lauded Advances in Medical Technology from the Global War on Terror

"If war is the dark side of humanity, then military medicine is the light."

—DR. JONATHAN WOODSON, ASSISTANT SECRETARY OF DEFENSE FOR HEALTH AFFAIRS

Tourniquets

Windlass, turnstile, the gate
latched to stave the wandering,
self-adhesive, twistage,
rod included, never at the joint.
Item of last resort, revolutionary,
one-handed operation,
the blooded grip, constriction,
door closed, the tap turned off,
the light intentionally dim.

Battlefield Dressing

From the carapace of lobsters
comes the stanching, clotting agent;
a full 50 percent perish out of want.
Morbidity versus mortality
and the words borne within:
morbid, mortal, moral,
as of a story with a less-than-happy
ending until the newest combat gauze,
from the Middle French *gaze*,
seen dimly, the curtain's descent,
chitosan so similar to our own
fingernails. Biodegradable, even.

Golden Hour Blood Container

Because heat or cold
is the ruin, slim window
of living, from this person
to that, from me to you,
one soldier born a universal donor,
another a universal recipient,
we say factors as if blood had a choice.
Treatment at the point of injury,
how a place is a field
before it is forever a battlefield.
Scraping away of the final boundary
of skin, the blood rising as it is wont.

Lozenge for Pain Management

The body taught to dampen
a nervous system overfull
of sympathies, learn to power down,
the soldier *cooperative and fully awake,*
candy to the tongue. Clip the wires,
reroute traffic, as if waterways,
as if the body were one long river
no longer touching its own banks,
left to run dry.

Prosthetics

Dancing With the Stars
made us believers.
Such leaps, see how
the civilians benefit. No longer
the frustration of zippers,

pennies in their slimness,
inclines as tricksters,
how the mind controls
and the digits obey, titanium,
lightweight, pinch process,
the algorithm of grasp and release.
Comes in all the tones that once
were called flesh.

Treating Traumatic Brain Injury

The signature wound of Iraq
and Afghanistan, concussive, small blast,
not a bruise exactly but a quake,
slosh in the bucket.
Hyperbaric oxygen therapy,
or was it hyperbola, loop
around the brain, the points
of anger running an endless track.
What we thought were stars:
cells winking out of existence.
Still unexplained: tinnitus,
the smallest of bells
ringing, ringing, ringing.
Slated for trials with children,
the danger of soccer and playgrounds
always a worry.

Regenerative Medicine

Who doesn't want to be reborn
after the flame, skin graft
sprayed like graffiti on a wall

blackened by soot, burn victim,
that great open wound.
Definitive coverage, how the skin
speaks in binary: here, not here
and the organs listen only to the skin.
Scars a map to nowhere, fading each day
until someone says, "Oh, were you
in the military?" and how startling,
how very good to be asked.

CNN Report: Symptoms of PTSD Mimic Lyme Disease

As if some bacteria had spiraled in,
hid in the closet, let the house fall asleep.
"The Great Imitator": even diseases

may put on camouflage, sit in shadow,
wait for orders. What of the droop
to the face, the heart's constant thrum,

the body overreacting, some rise
in temperature, some flush as if kissed,
who left the lights on, the lights

aren't on. Hand to the throat:
any yelling may be your own.
Sweating: unlike panting, impossible

to control. Night terrors, day terrors,
thrash on the couch, unbelievable,
unbelieved. Stop moping, get out more,

all in your head, you're home now,
you're safe, family to consider,
the meds, the weight gain,

the loss, the breathless, the rasp of it.
No magic bullet: tell me about it.
Sometimes a rash like a target

.   .   .

so loved by marksmen.
Despite everything, breath goes out
and is pulled back in.

Details Emerge of Bowe Bergdahl Captivity

Walls the fingernails scratch.
Lines merge into pictures
only he can see in the yellowing.

A house falling, torn into sand.
Birdish skeletons, grasshoppers
with their legs scattered,

bending the wrong way.
Teeth in the mouth let go their grip.
Or the gums go soft. He doesn't pry.

Two hands forget how to hold,
forget to reach across
and find each other in the dark.

Food, what little.
The body itself a spoon.
The body a tongue barely moist,

the joints stretching and taste.
If Bowe could run how he would,
and the wind, how that would taste

against his lips, inside the mouth,
across the narrow of his thighs.
His bones rattling in their husk.

One life's worth? I wouldn't guess.
Don't say ragged, down to the quick.
Don't point out the bloody obvious.

Wright-Patterson Air Force Base:
Intercontinental Ballistic Missiles

Our son touches
them. The guards
don't mind.

Relics from a time
when nuclear
was everything.

Minuteman,
Peacekeeper,
Jupiter, Thor.

The ICBMs
six stories tall,
stunningly phallic.

The best offer
"enhanced survivability
during nuclear strike."

These things
can't hurt you,
one guard says,

not anymore.
He raps a knuckle
to test the ring.

. . .

Knows just
the spots
for certain notes.

Has musical background.
Loves jazz.
Heard of Chet Baker?

The low notes are Titan I.
High notes from
the shorter Minuteman.

When the crowd thins
he plays "Do-Re-Mi" and "Here
Comes the Bride," only slow,

like a funeral dirge,
because of the distance
between notes.

Sergeant: *Origin* < one who serves

By medieval standards
worth half a knight,
valet who knows
both ends of the sword
or the nock in an arrow,
knows when to hold
his tongue. If a man tasked
to fight for fields not his,
if a man told he was worth
half a knight, told to act
as a shield, the subservience,
the dipped head, the birthright,
the damned at birth, if a man.
If one who serves then hold
the door, shine another
man's shoes, tend his horse,
treat it as he would his own,
treat it better, the lord's horse,
if a man. Worth half a knight
the man, uptake of arms
a castle not his own,
subordinate, contracted *m'lord*
a squeeze at the throat,
sergeant, *servire*, the horse
reins held, the human shield
worth half a knight.
Hold the platter, hold
the tongue, serve the meal.
A word's lineage: *servise*
the Anglo-French from Latin

servitium, condition of a slave
from *servus*, the slave's body
as if a man had only
the body, as if a human shield.
Later, collect the stripped bones,
the napkins greased. Consider
a tankard cut in half,
how little it expects
to hold.

Rescued Parrots Used in PTSD Therapy

Before Serenity Park these birds
self-mutilated: featherpluck, bloodbeak,
broken. Through the compound
a veteran runs the damaged birds:
You're flying! You're flying!
Though this lorikeet will never fly again,
tangle of birdskin and buzzsaw,
it flaps as if complicit in the ruse.
A marine lines with battered birds
his wheelchair. The tank gunner
an expert on sunflower seeds given
from lips to curving beaks.
The parrots know who's who and have
their favorites. One loves a sailor.
A macaw sings only for Jim.
The sulfur-crested cockatoo
chooses the helicopter pilot:
Never has a bird let me down.
One parrot spends each morning
yelling *Shut up or else!*
in the only cage the vets
won't approach before noon.
These birds are hurting,
Matt says, his good arm
sweeping the whole of the park.
Some vets won't talk unless
a bird's close by. Some clean
the aviary, weeping. Some parrots
can't be with another bird, consider
themselves human, or near enough.

Nocturne with Tracers

If in my memory
the tracers
no longer reddened
the nightfall and hush,
I could love the Army
a little less.

In every foxhole
one woman next to
one woman
and the smell
of gun oil which is
an aphrodisiac.

Every soldier had
her battle buddy.
We whispered
as if one were
the other's secret.

It was the night
wanting us
to whisper.
Along the foxholes,
the murmuration
of women.

Tracers a necklace
of light. Lips to my
ear she'd tell me

You're on target,
you've got this
in a voice so soft
it was barely Army.

It's hard to take that girl seriously
even with the gun.
Her grip tightens to white.
Everyone in the platoon held
the same gun, sat in front of
the same flag, put on a War Face.
Is War Face with Perm possible?
The muscles of the face
not always under her control.
Skeeter wing insignia:
as low as you can go,
of multitudes, insignificant,
insectal, chum for predators.
Lifting the eyes a struggle:
we'd spent weeks not looking
at drill sergeants' faces.
The gun meant to give power.
Drill sergeants to take it away.
Her face: porcelain glaze,
dinnerplate, milk bland,
wedge of lips. I could put
my thumb over this picture,
erase her completely.

Army SMART Book: This Page Left Blank Intentionally

Soldiers come home with sand
in their bellies, or nothing at all.

Faces crumpling
like sheets of paper.

Here's the best advice I got on the range:
make the mind whitewalled,

room with no furniture, high noon,
heat rippled. Make it sunstroke and still.

Let the breath out. Squeeze.
See what the bullet writes down.

Discharge: *Origin* < *Latin*, to run away

Not quite the opposite of *charge*
but close enough. Backpedal, a drift
toward the door, six weeks and a wake-up,
sign this form, sign this form.
What the Army lets you keep:
BDU cap, T-shirts. The shoeshine kit
was always yours as is the flask.
Unroll the sleeves, unshine the boots,
razor the name tag's stitches,
remove the rank. If male, consider
a whole new pattern of facial hair.
If female, an Afro, goddess braids, hair
that won't be contained or its opposite:
slick skin, buzz cut, butch.
Tattoo on the neck or knuckles:
thinking about it. What's done
may be undone. See the doctor,
see the dentist, have the tooth pulled,
accept the college brochures.
Take the aptitude tests,
fill in the bubbles, can you write,
can you subtract, divide what remains,
drive for long hours, love the smell
of the motor pool, get along with others;
do you escalate or de-escalate,
scare when fireworks,
sit with back to the wall,
avoid crowds, avoid intimacy,
feel the tinder inside, strike the match,
have a place to go. If hometown, where.

If family. If bank account.
If bus ticket. Keep the duffel bag.
Keep the cap pulled low.
At first, anyone stepping into sunshine
will say it's too bright.

Civil War Reenactment, Look Park, Massachusetts

The bridge needs defending,
choke point between swing sets
and water park. A gray soldier

tells me not to go beyond
the picnic tables. A stealthy
Union man checks his phone.

We're front seat, lunch spread out,
and while the battle rages
I eat cold corn on the cob,

which always takes a while
and requires looking down to see
what's been consumed.

Children, there's watermelon. They eat
watermelon. A man beside a tree crumples.
Another fixes a bayonet.

I tell them what I know of war,
the battle charge to come. They want to know
why you don't hold bayonets like knives.

I say, to keep your distance.
Still so close
the distance between two bodies.

. . .

I don't say, for leverage.
To drive the bayonet deeper,
to force the point into the stomach of a man.

The firing stops. The yells of men and boys.
When two grapple and one falls dead,
I look back to my corn, which I've neglected.

Later they'll help each other up, brush
each other off, but in the charge I heard them
wanting.

At the First Battle of Bull Run,
spectators dressed up.
Women with opera glasses. Women

selling pies. Far enough away
that when the big artillery began,
they applauded, sure the war

would be contained in one weekend,
in this bowl
of grass and stone.

Later we ride the kiddie train,
through the tents of soldiers and civilians
in knickers and long skirts.

Look, they took their kids! my two
exclaim, glad. The tracks hairpin
by the amputation demo.

. . .

I remind them about starvation and disease.
My daughter wants to know
about dysentery, smallpox.

Yellow fever! She likes the sound
of this. Her favorite color's yellow.
The train rumbles through a tunnel.

Beyond it, men in gray—bandits, rebels—
are set to rob the train.
The children clutch

play coins given in advance
and hand them gleefully to a smiling man.
The children are not scared

and the children are not scared
and when I say you know this is not
what real war is like they say I know, I know

and when the train stops
they run off to feed the deer
behind the bars.

Sayler's Creek Battlefield

You here for the hummingbird talk?
the ranger asks. It's 102 degrees
and the visitor's center has AC.

Over battlefield relics, the ranger's taped
pictures of delicate nests, a whir of birds.
Jewel to the throat. Behind them,

Minié balls hover, never reaching a target.
He recommends the driving tour,
radio set to 1610.

I drive the last major battleground
of the Army of Northern Virginia,
just days before surrender.

Thousands died not knowing
that in 150 years the streets would bear
cheerful signs: "Lee's Retreat"

with a cartoon bugle. The radio crackles.
The corn's grown tall again
and there are cows, generations

from the cows Confederate troops ate,
raw, so faint from hunger cooking
wouldn't do. Even hummingbirds

can't cover what's been done.
A commemorative painting dark enough
I can't tell blue from gray, and maybe

. . .

that was true in life. Because
of AM propagation and Virginia hills
a ghost voice fades out, comes back,

telling me what happened here
but it's so faint it might be telling me
the thing that's still to come.

NOTES

"Origin" poems: My dictionary of choice is Merriam Webster, both print and online. Additional information and etymological wanderings I owe to wordsmith.org and etymonline.com.

"Army SMART Book" poems are indebted, in part, to the *Soldiers' Manual, Army Training* book, now called the *Soldier's Manual of Common Tasks, Warrior Skills Level I,* given to all recruits. All quoted material is taken from versions of this book.

"Combined Plow and Gun Patent, 1862": From U.S. patent number 35,600, issued June 1862: "This combination enables those in agricultural pursuits to have at hand an efficient weapon of defense."

"'The Great Sacrifice of the Romans on Undertaking a War'" is an engraving that appears in *The Faiths of the World: A Dictionary of All Religions and Religious Sects,* by Reverend James Gardner.

"Soldiers' 'Fun' Photo with Flag-Draped Coffin Sparks Outrage": The title was taken from the 2014 headline at NPR.org.

"Chevron: *Origin* < rafter, *also* goat": "slick sleeve" refers to newly enlisted soldiers at the lowest pay grade as they have no sleeve or collar insignia yet. The rafter and rocker refer to the most common elements of the rank insignias. Occasionally, soldiers are promoted before entering basic training; "blackened wingtips" refers to the collar insignia for this next-lowest pay grade and rank, E2/PV2.

"Manassas": This Civil War battlefield and battles were named "Manassas" by the Confederates, for the Virginia city, and "Bull Run" by the Union, for the river nearby. I've used both terms in this book.

"Most Lauded Advances in Medical Technology from the Global War on Terror": Information for this poem and all italicized phrases were taken from the 2014 article "10 Advances in Medical Technology from the Global War on Terror" in *Task & Purpose.*

"Details Emerge of Bowe Bergdahl Captivity": Some information for this poem and much of the title is from the 2014 *New York Times* article "As Bowe Bergdahl Heals, Details Emerge of His Captivity."

"Rescued Parrots Used in PTSD Therapy": Inspiration and some information for this poem came from the 2016 *New York Times* article "What Does a Parrot Know About PTSD?"

"Company B Graduation Booklet: PV2 Skolfield": "Skeeter wings" is slang for the single chevron of the PV2 insignia. With thanks to my ranger buddy Herbie for digging up this photo and for always having my six.

"Discharge: *Origin < Latin,* to run away": BDU stands for Battle Dress Uniform, the standard-issue uniform from the 1980s to the mid-2000s.

"Sayler's/Sailor's Creek Battlefield." There's some disagreement about the spelling, with local, state, and national park services and tradition on different sides. To honor this, I use "Sayler" in the poem itself and "Sailor" in the Table of Contents.

ACKNOWLEDGMENTS

Grateful acknowledgment is made to the editors of the following publications where these poems first appeared:

32 Poems: "Discharge: *Origin < Latin*, to run away," "War: *Origin < Old German*, to confuse"

Alaska Quarterly Review: "Anticipate Gunshots in the Second Half of the Play"

Another Chicago Magazine: "Third Platoon Learns Cover & Concealment"

As You Were: The Military Review: "CNN Report: Rise in Sexual Assaults, Reprisals in the Military (2016)," "Wright-Patterson Air Force Base: Intercontinental Ballistic Missiles"

Calyx: "We Invaded Two Weeks Later"

CONSEQUENCE Magazine: "Details Emerge of Bowe Bergdahl Captivity," "Poem with the Moment the Infantry Unit Is Given Clearance to Shoot Children"

Crab Orchard Review: "Soldiers' 'Fun' Photo with Flag-Draped Coffin Sparks Outrage"

Crazyhorse: "Rifle: *verb, noun*"

Cutthroat: "Wyoming Field Tactics"

Guernica: "Army SMART Book Section 1-8: 'The origin of the hand salute is uncertain'"

Indiana Review: "Army SMART Book: M18A1 Claymore Mine"

Iowa Review: "Army SMART Book: Inspirational Quotes (I)," "Army SMART Book: Inspirational Quotes (II)," "'The Great Sacrifice of the Romans on Undertaking a War,'" "Rescued Parrots Used in PTSD Therapy," "Why I Never Wrote About the Army"

MIRAMAR: "Concertina Wire: *Origin < from* concert," "Nocturne with Tracers"

Missouri Review: "Company B Graduation Booklet: PV2 Skolfield," "Grenade: *Origin < OFr.* pomme-grenate," "Private, PV2, Private First Class," "The Throwing Gap"

Ploughshares: "Enlist: *Origin < German,* to court, to woo"

Plume Poetry: "Bayonet: *Origin < from* Bayonne, France," "Sergeant: *Origin <* one who serves"

RHINO: "On Veterans Day, My Daughter Wishes Me Happy Veterinarians Day"

Shenandoah: "Classic Green Army Figures Give Up Guns for Yoga"

Slice: "Combined Plow and Gun Patent, 1862," "Army SMART Book: 'Small-Arms Fire May Sound Like Mosquitoes'"

Southeast Missouri State University Press (*Proud to Be: Writing by American Warriors* anthology): "Army SMART Book: This Page Left Blank Intentionally"

Sugar House Review: "Chevron: *Origin <* rafter, *also* goat," "Due to Historical Accuracy, Hazards Are Present"

Third Coast: "Army SMART Book: Identification Tags, with Silencers"

Tupelo Quarterly: "Double Arm Transplant"

UCity Review: "Manassas"

Valparaiso Poetry Review: "Most Lauded Advances in Medical Technology from the Global War on Terror," "Sayler's Creek Battlefield," "Soldier Rendered as All Five Types of Sand Dunes"

Waccamaw: "Civil War Reenactment, Look Park, Massachusetts"

Special thanks to Hedgebrook, the Massachusetts Cultural Council, the *Missouri Review,* the *Iowa Review,* Ucross Foundation, Vermont Studio Center, and the Virginia Center for the Creative Arts for additional support during the writing of this book.

Manuscript readers, this book would not exist without your help and full-on enthusiasm: Brandon Amico, Kristin Bock, Janet Bowdan. For feedback along the way, additional thanks to Tricia Asklar, Corwin Ericson, Daniel Hales, Adam Houle, Janel Nockelby, Susan Schultz.